LET'S GET MOVING!

W9-BPR-429

You Can Be an Ice-Skater

Alix Wood

Gareth Stevens
Publishing

Please visit our website, **www.garethstevens.com**. For a free color catalog of all our high-quality books, call toll free 1-800-542-2595 or fax 1-877-542-2596

Library of Congress Cataloging-in-Publication Data

Wood, Alix.
You can be an ice-skater / by Alix Wood.
 p. cm. — (Let's get moving!)
Includes index.
ISBN 978-1-4824-0284-1 (pbk.)
ISBN 978-1-4824-0286-5 (6-pack)
ISBN 978-1-4824-0283-4 (library binding)
1. Skating — Juvenile literature. 2. Figure skating — Juvenile literature. I. Wood, Alix. II. Title.
GV849.W66 2014
796.91—dc23

First Edition

Published in 2014 by
Gareth Stevens Publishing
111 East 14th Street, Suite 349
New York, NY 10003

© Alix Wood Books

Produced for Gareth Stevens by Alix Wood Books
Designed by Alix Wood
Art direction and content research: Kevin Wood
Editor: Eloise Macgregor
Consultant: Deborah Marsh

Photo credits:
Cover, 1, 3, 4, 26 bottom © Shutterstock; 23 bottom © Olga Besnard/Shutterstock;
© 28 top © Marcello Farina/Shutterstock; 29 top © Vladislav Gajic/Shutterstock;
29 bottom © Diego Barbieri/Shutterstock; 28 bottom © Luka Mall; all other photos
© Greg Dennis

Acknowledgments
With grateful thanks to skaters Chloe White, Georgia Bennett, Elliott Rowe, Jake Psaras, and Jack Pethard

Printed in the United States of America

CPSIA compliance information: Batch #CW14GS: For further information contact Gareth Stevens, New York, New York at 1-800-542-2595.

Contents

Why Ice-Skate?

Skating helps improve your balance and **coordination**. It keeps you flexible and builds your leg muscles. Ice-skating develops your concentration, memory skills, and **spatial awareness**. And it's fun!

Ice-skating is very sociable. Many cities have ice rinks, and many towns have pop-up ice rinks in the winter months. It's fun to go with friends and try to skate. Never skate on a frozen lake or pond however. It can be very dangerous if the ice breaks.

These girls are skating on a specially made outdoor ice rink.

Fitting your ice skates

You can usually rent ice skates at a rink. Make sure you tie your skates properly. Don't tie them too loose, but also not so tight that it cuts off your blood circulation. Keep your skate guards on and try walking in them on the rubber matting. Your toes should just touch the front cap of the skates, and the skate should be snug enough so that your heel does not lift off the bottom.

You don't need to buy special clothes to ice-skate. Wear clothes that are easy to move around in and will not get heavy when wet.

Warm thick leggings or sweatpants, a long-sleeved T-shirt, and gloves are ideal for the ice. It can get cold so take a jacket, too. Avoid loose-fitting pants as your ice skate blades could get caught in the legs and make you trip.

Go to the entry door and take off your skate guards if you have them on. You are ready to try to skate.

When you get on the ice, skate in the same direction as everyone else. Don't try skating the wrong way around the ice rink as you may end up hurting other people and possibly yourself. To start with, walk around the edge of the rink while holding on to the wall. This will help you get a feel for the ice. Start slow and avoid jerky movements.

Try not to stiffen your body, as that actually makes skating harder. If you can learn to balance yourself while going slower, moving faster will seem easy. The faster you go, the easier it is to balance. Once you feel confident, try moving away from the edge.

Once you are on the ice try to lift up one foot and then the other. Once you can do this, try to take about four small "baby steps" and then stop and glide on two feet.

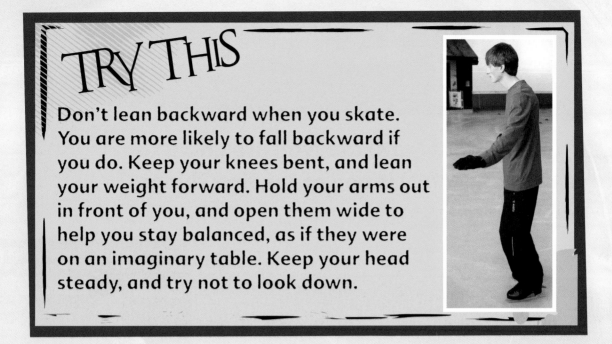

TRY THIS

Don't lean backward when you skate. You are more likely to fall backward if you do. Keep your knees bent, and lean your weight forward. Hold your arms out in front of you, and open them wide to help you stay balanced, as if they were on an imaginary table. Keep your head steady, and try not to look down.

Before you skate, you should warm up your muscles slowly. Skating takes place in a cold arena, so your muscles are going to be cold to start with. Stretching in a cold environment can lead to muscle tears, so warm up well. Once you can skate, a good way to warm up is to get on the ice and do a few gentle laps of the rink.

In this skating class, the students warm up by doing some simple turns and laps of the ice rink. This gently works all the muscles they will need for the session.

Falling Is Fun

If you are going to skate, you are going to fall! Falling safely is one of the first things you need to learn.

Falling means you're learning. You shouldn't be afraid of it. Even the most experienced skaters will fall when they try new skills. Knowing how to fall safely will make you more confident on the ice.

When you feel you are starting to fall, bend your knees and squat into a dip position.

Ease yourself down toward the ice.

Keep your hands up and your fists clenched.

Fall to the side and lean forward as you fall.

Getting Up

1

Quickly get onto your knees.

2

Lift one knee and place both hands on it. Push yourself up using your knee as a base.

TRY THIS

How To Fall Safely

Put your hands in the air or on your lap when you fall. If you leave your hands on the ice, another skater could skate over your fingers! If you do need to push yourself up using your hands, make them into fists. Wearing gloves and wrist guards will keep you from getting hurt. Elbow and knee pads are a good idea as well. When you fall, land on the side seam of your pants. If you wobble try immediately putting your hands on your knees. This keeps your arms from flailing around and may keep you from falling.

Gliding and Stopping

Once you have learned how to balance and how to fall, it's time to learn how to skate and stop more gracefully.

Gliding on one foot is a basic skating move that all figure skaters must learn and master. It is also the basis for gliding from foot to foot to get around the rink.

Start your glide by putting your feet in a "T" shape. Use your back foot to push off from.

As you begin to glide forward, shift your weight to your front foot, and slowly lift your back leg.

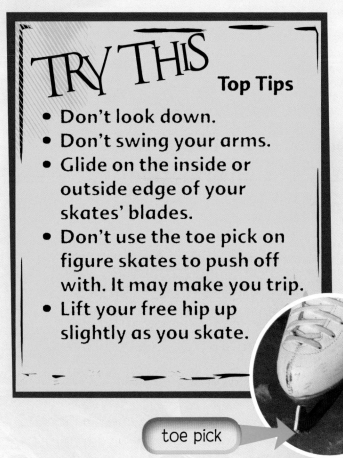

TRY THIS   Top Tips

- Don't look down.
- Don't swing your arms.
- Glide on the inside or outside edge of your skates' blades.
- Don't use the toe pick on figure skates to push off with. It may make you trip.
- Lift your free hip up slightly as you skate.

toe pick

Once you can glide on one foot, try stroking. Stroking means moving from one skate to the other. Begin with your feet in a T position. Do a one foot glide. Then move from one foot to the other. Your free leg should be extended behind you with your toe pointed. Your skating knee should be bent. Start with short, quick glides before you try to balance on one leg for a long time.

Now try to do a dip. In a dip a skater squats down as far as possible. The arms and rear should be level. This is a great exercise for your knees and your balance. First, practice doing a dip from a standstill. Once you feel comfortable, practice dips while gliding forward on two feet.

A perfectly controlled dip

Stopping

There are several different ways to stop on the ice, apart from falling over! The T-stop, V-stop, and hockey stop are all effective methods of coming to a halt.

The first stop most beginner skaters learn is the V-stop, or snowplow stop. It can be done with both feet or with one foot. Most skaters favor one foot or the other for stopping.

The V-Stop
Skate slowly with your knees bent slightly. Point your toes inward to make a "V" shape with your feet. You should gradually come to a stop. Practice going a little faster.

TRY THIS

The V-stop must be done on the flat center of the blade, not the edges. Practice pushing the flat of the blade out while holding onto the rail. There should be some **friction**, and some ice shavings should form.

The snowplow stop is not very elegant. Many figure skaters do a T-stop instead. The skater's feet make the shape of a "T" on the ice. The back foot does the actual stopping as it scrapes the ice with the back outside edge.

The T-stop

While skating slowly, bring your left foot behind your right blade at right angles. Your left foot should start to drag on the outside edge of its blade behind the back tip of your right blade. You will start to slow down and then stop. Make sure you use the outside edge of your blade, or you will go around in circles!

The Hockey Stop

Skate slowly with your knees bent slightly. When you are ready quickly turn one skate to any side. It's a good idea to learn how to stop on both sides. When you turn your feet sideways, you should push your feet into the ice to have a quicker, faster, and sharper stop.

When ice hockey players do a hockey stop they usually do it using two feet. The front blade is pressed to the inside edge, and the back foot fits right behind the front foot on the outside edge. Both knees bend. Pressure is towards the front part of the blades.

Forward and Backward

One way to start skating forward is by doing short "scooter" steps with one foot at a time.

Pretend you are riding a scooter down the street. Hold you arms in front for balance. Do alternating "scooter" steps. Try skating around the rink on your imaginary scooter, pushing with alternate legs.

TRY THIS

There's no need for fancy footwork when you want to turn. You can steer with your shoulders. Turn your outside shoulder (the one farthest from the direction you want to turn) forward and you will start to turn.

Take a step on your right foot.

Glide on two feet. Try taking a step with your left foot.

You can learn to glide backward. Be careful to head in the direction of everyone else on the rink when you do. Keep one eye looking over your shoulder to see where you are going.

Practice walking backward on the ice first. Then try taking baby steps, then gliding with both feet.

The more you push with the front of your feet, the more speed you will pick up. Push out with your knees.

Stand with your feet forming a "V" shape.

Push your feet apart. Make little half circles with the insides of your **skates** while moving backward.

Make a circle with the other foot.

Turning and Jumping

Once you've mastered the basics of ice-skating, you can try out some jumps and turns.

Different ways of turning suit different purposes. Crossovers are great for quickly skating around a corner, and would be used by figure skaters, hockey players, and speed skaters. More graceful gliding turns would be used mainly by figure skaters.

To perform a simple gliding turn, start gliding forward on two feet. Keep your feet close together.

Turn your upper body in the direction you want to turn. Don't let your hips and legs follow. Lean into the turn. This will put you on the edges of your blades.

Bend your left knee. Skate on a left outside edge and right inside edge. Bring your right shoulder around.

Crossovers are another way ice skaters move around corners. On a curve, the skater crosses the outside skate over the skate that is on the inside of the curve.

1

2

3

Put your feet together, and line up your hips and shoulders right over your feet. Bend your knees.

Skate forward, and cross your right foot over your left foot. Skate from a left forward outside edge to a right forward inside edge.

Keep both feet pointing in the same direction. Return the feet back to a parallel position and begin again.

TRY THIS

Crossover Tips

Crossovers are a little like walking sideways up a set of spiral stairs. The key to crossovers is to lean into the circle. The faster you go, the farther in you will have to lean to keep your balance. Leaning into the circle will make you glide on the edges of your blades. Your inner leg will be on the outside edge, and your crossing leg will be on the inside edge. Practice going around in both directions.

Ice-skating jumps are either toe jumps or edge jumps. For toe jumps, you plant your toe pick into the ice for the take off. For edge jumps you use a knee bend, which tips your weight forward towards the toe pick for the take off. Edge jumps don't involve any toe pick movement. Instead, skaters use only their **momentum** and leg and foot muscles to leap powerfully into the air, usually from one foot.

A Jump and Turn

Skate at a moderate speed. Bend your knees. Take off from the inside edge of one skate. Do a half turn in the air, using your arms to propel yourself around. Land on your other ice skate on the outside edge.

TRY THIS

Try doing this drag. Move your right leg forward and dip so your left leg is low. Keep your shoulders level and your drag leg behind you, not to one side. The inside of your boot should touch the ice. Your weight is on your front leg. You could try and glide around a corner using a forward drag.

Wear skates with a good ankle support, as you will land heavily.

The Waltz Jump

The waltz jump is sometimes also called the 3-jump. You make the shape of the number three on the ice if you do the jump correctly.

It's a good idea to do some backward glides on one foot (page 10) to practice the landing position before you try this jump.

1

2

3

Push and glide on your left leg with your left leg slightly bent and your right leg stretched out behind you.

Start to kick your right leg up so your right knee goes up in the air in front of you.

As you start the take off, leave the ice on your left toe pick.

TRY THIS

Clockwise, or counterclockwise?

Try doing the waltz jump off the ice first to get a feel of the move. You may not feel comfortable doing the jump starting on your left foot and landing on your right. This turns you in an counterclockwise direction. If you prefer to turn the other way, you can reverse these instructions and start on your right foot and land on your left.

4 **5** **6**

If you are in the right starting position you will automatically make a half rotation.

Landing on your right toe pick, roll down to a flat blade on your back outside edge of your right foot.

Then skate on your right leg with your left leg extended behind you, gliding backward.

Ice Dancing

Ice dancing is a mixture of figure skating and ballroom dancing. It is a fun way to keep fit and use your new ice-skating skills.

Ice dancing competitions normally contain three different elements. Compulsory routines follow a set pattern of steps. Original routines allow the dancers to choose the music and the moves but are to a set rhythm. Free routines allow the skater to choose the rhythm, too.

Killian position is a basic skating position that figure skating partners use in both ice dancing and pair skating.

Killian Position

The man holds his partner's left hand with his left hand while standing slightly behind and left of her. He puts his right hand on his partner's right hip. She places and holds her right hand on and around the man's right hand. When the woman stands to the left of the man, the team is skating in reverse Killian position.

Ready to dance!

A spiral is when a skater puts their right or left leg in the air and balances on the other leg.

Spiral
Skate at a medium speed. Balance on the foot that you will spiral with. Put your other leg out behind you. Put your hands out or parallel with the leg behind you. You may also hold up your back leg with your hands.

TRY THIS

Get the right shoes. Ice dancers' blades are about an inch shorter at the back than those used by other skaters. This is to allow for **intricate** footwork and close skating. They also have a smaller pick. The most common colors for skates are black for men and white for women.

The Novice Foxtrot

The novice foxtrot is a basic dance that is good to learn as a beginner. You can dance it on your own or with a partner.

With ice dancing, timing is important. The first step of the dance has to be on the correct bar of the music. An instructor would have to help you get the timing right.

1

If you have a partner, hold them in Killian (see page 22).

2

Push off from your left leg, then right, then left, then right.

You will need to circle around the ice rink now or you'll hit the wall, so do two crossovers for two beats of the music. Push forward and then swing back your right leg for four beats of the music. Then swing it forward for four beats. Now do three more crossovers.

TRY THIS

You need to be aware of how big your rink is and where your turns should happen so you miss the walls!

Push, then do a left leg swing back for four beats.

Then, do a left leg swing forward for four beats.

Ice Hockey

Ice hockey is a team sport played on ice. Skaters use sticks to shoot a hard rubber hockey puck into their opponent's net to score points.

Hockey skates are very different from figure skates. They must be rigid and tough to protect the skater's feet from contact with other skaters. The short light blade on hockey skates helps players with speed and quick stops.

TRY THIS

During an ice hockey game, players must wear a helmet, protective pads and gloves, and a mouth guard. It's a good idea to practice skating while wearing the clothing.

The Slap Shot

Point your feet toward the puck, which should be about 3 feet (1 m) away from your skates. Holding the stick, your right hand should be shoulder width apart from your left hand. Lift your stick to waist height.

Make contact with the ice just before you hit the puck. This helps flex your stick and will shoot the puck faster.

As you lift your stick to follow through the shot, aim the stick toward where you are aiming the puck. Your shoulders, your hips, and your front foot should all twist toward the direction of the shot.

Speed Skating

Speed skating is a competitive form of ice skating in which the competitors race each other over a certain distance on skates.

The standard rink for speed skating is a quarter of a mile (400 m) long! When people race on a standard ice hockey rink, that is called "short track." Short track involves a lot of fast cornering.

short track

long track

Speed skaters wear tight fitting clothing to make them as **aerodynamic** as possible. Most professionals wear a special skin suit made of stretchy swimsuit-type fabric. As a beginner, just wear any tight-fitting clothing that you can still move easily in.

Try Speed Skating

Stand in a low crouched position. Keep your skate on the ice for as long as possible as you push out to the side. Place one arm behind your back to minimize drag. Do crossovers around the corners, and swing your outside arm to help with **acceleration**. Remember to push from heel to toe. This gives you better control over your skates.

TRY THIS

Glove Tips

Many short track speed skaters touch the ice with their left hand finger tips while skating through the turns. You can buy special speed skating gloves, or some people buy special fingertip covers for their own gloves which they glue on to protect the tips.

Glossary

acceleration An increase in speed.

aerodynamic Having a shape that reduces the drag from air moving past.

coordination Parts working together smoothly, such as in good muscular coordination.

friction The force that resists motion between bodies in contact, such as the friction of a box sliding along the floor.

intricate Having many complexly interrelating parts, or elements.

momentum The characteristic of a moving body that is caused by its mass and its motion.

spatial awareness One's ability to perceive and understand the relationship between shapes and areas around them.

For More Information

Books

Cheung, Ben. *How to Ice Skate: Beginner's Guide.* Amazon Digital Services, 2012.

Gustaitis, Joseph. *Speed Skating.* New York, NY: Crabtree Publishing, 2010.

Gustaitis, Joseph. *Figure Skating.* New York, NY: Crabtree Publishing, 2009.

Websites

Kid's World
www.kidzworld.com/article/5204-figure-skating
This website has a short history, skating terms, and links to skate-related topics.

How to Ice Skate

www.wikihow.com/Ice-Skate
Read information for beginner ice skaters.

Publisher's note to educators and parents: Our editors have carefully reviewed these websites to ensure that they are suitable for students. Many websites change frequently, however, and we cannot guarantee that a site's future contents will continue to meet our high standards of quality and educational value. Be advised that students should be closely supervised whenever they access the Internet.

Index